# Sports Illustrated KIDS

# FOOTBALL Opposites

BY MARK WEAKLAND

CAPSTONE PRESS
a capstone imprint

Sports Illustrated Kids Rookie Books are published by Capstone Press,
1710 Roe Crest Drive, North Mankato, Minnesota 56003
www.capstonepub.com

**Library of Congress Cataloging-in-Publication Data**
Cataloging-in-publication information is on file with the Library of Congress.
ISBN 978-1-4296-9960-0 (library binding)


**Editorial Credits**
Jeni Wittrock, editor; Juliette Peters, designer; Eric Gohl, media researcher;
Eric Manske, production specialist


**Photo Credits**
Shutterstock: David Lee, 1, Ken Durden, 4; *Sports Illustrated*: Bob Rosato, 13, 14, 15, 16–17,
23, Damian Strohmeyer, 8, 11, 12, 18, 19, 29, David E. Klutho, cover, Heinz Kluetmeier, 20,
John Biever, 3, 5, 24, 25, 26, John W. McDonough, 9, 28, Peter Read Miller, 6–7, 22, Robert
Beck, 27, Simon Bruty, 10, 21

Printed in the United States of America in North Mankato, Minnesota.
092012    006933CGS13

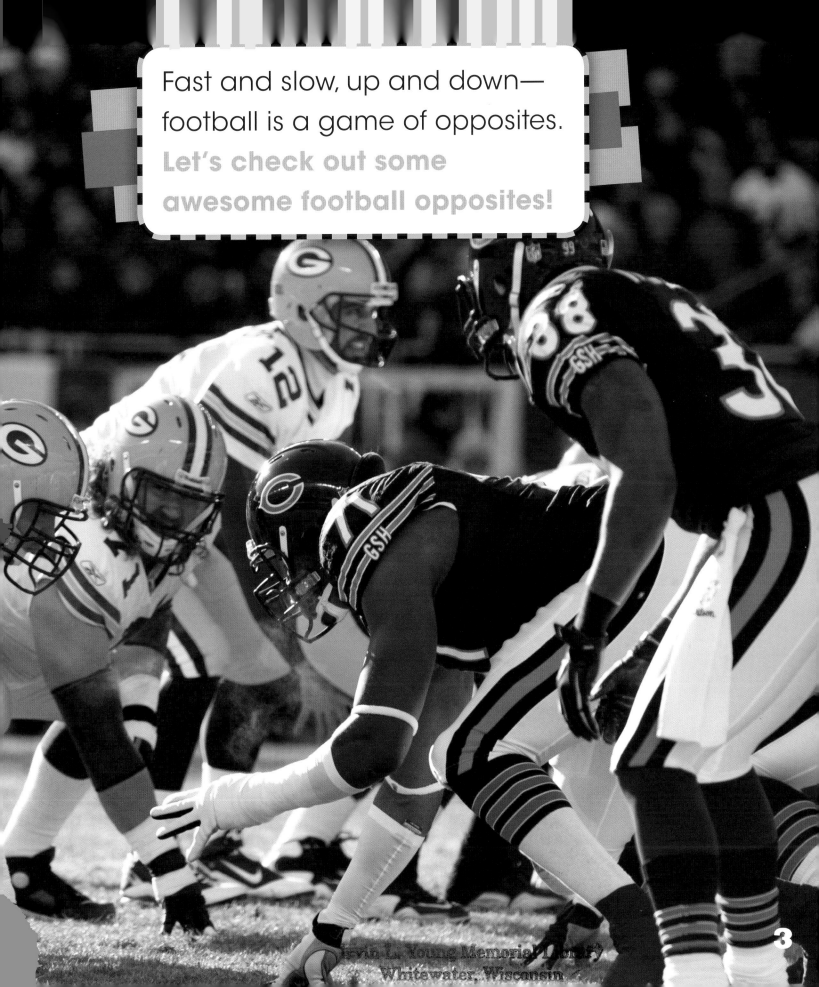

Fast and slow, up and down—
football is a game of opposites.
Let's check out some
awesome football opposites!

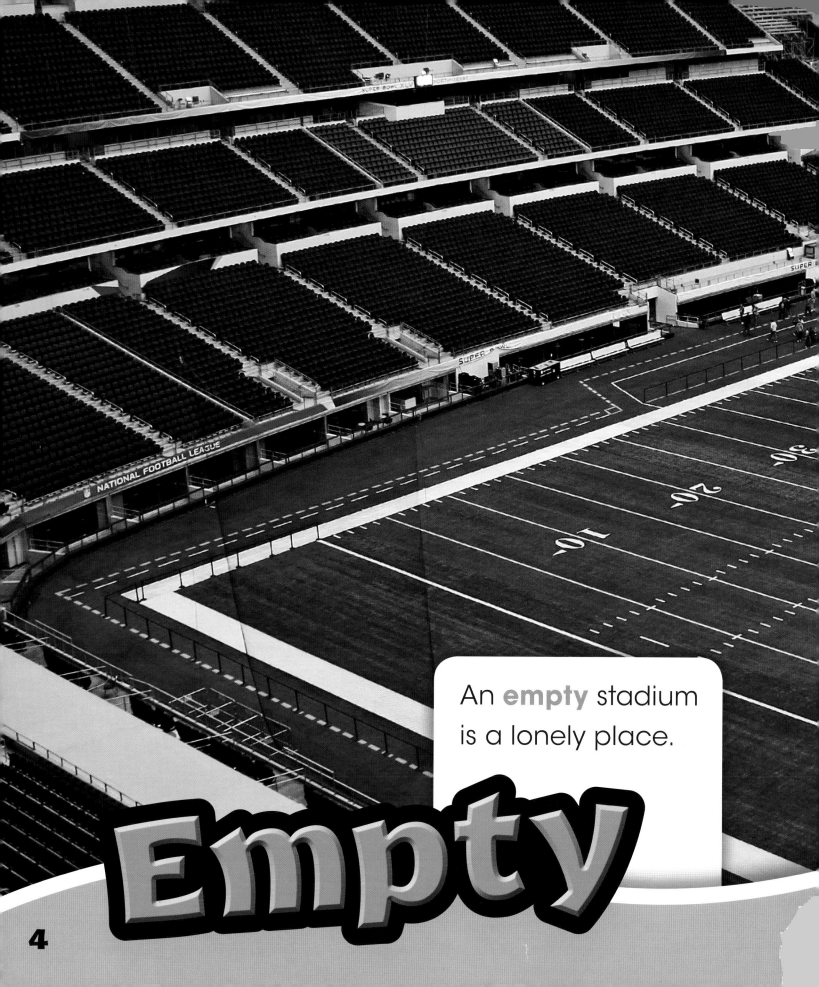

An **empty** stadium is a lonely place.

Empty

# Full

On game day the stadium is full of excited fans.

A football field is long.
One goalpost is **near**.

Near

# Far

The opposite post is **far** away. How far? Exactly 120 yards (110 meters).

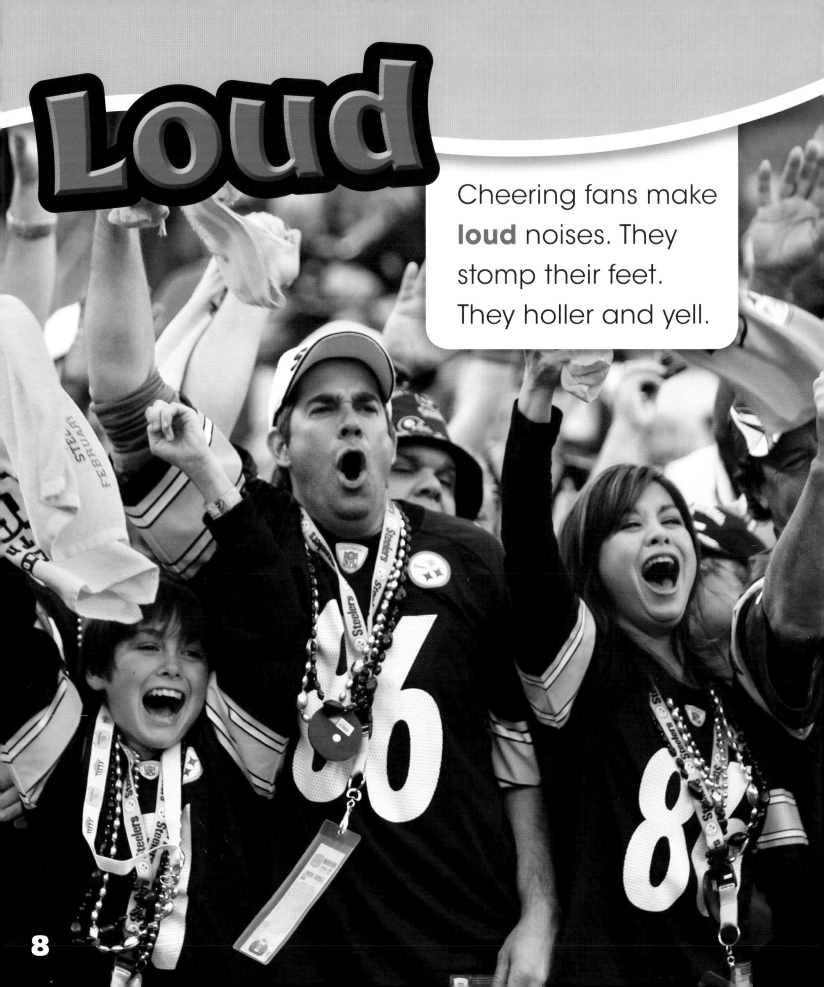

# Loud

Cheering fans make **loud** noises. They stomp their feet. They holler and yell.

Players also come crashing down. Look out!

# Down

Is he a bird? Is he a plane? No! He is a football player leaping **over** others to score a touchdown.

Over

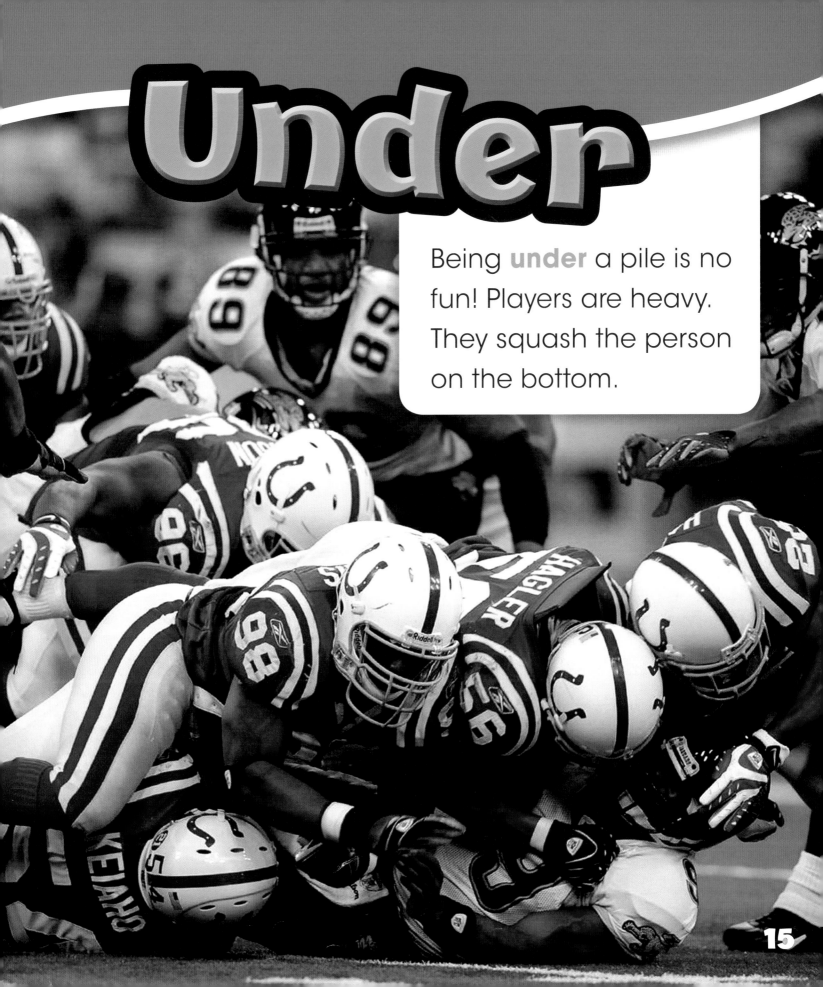

# Under

Being **under** a pile is no fun! Players are heavy. They squash the person on the bottom.

Big

Little

**Big** players tower over **little** ones.
But the little ones are quick and tough.
Big or small, every player wants to win.

# Day

Football is played day and night. During the **day** sunlight shines on outdoor stadiums.

At **night**, bright lights
beam down on the field.

Night

# Fast

A running back speeds by in a blur. He is **fast**!

Players help an injured teammmate. It is a **slow** march off the field.

Slow

# Clean

There's no dirt or mud on this player. His **clean** uniform is spotless.

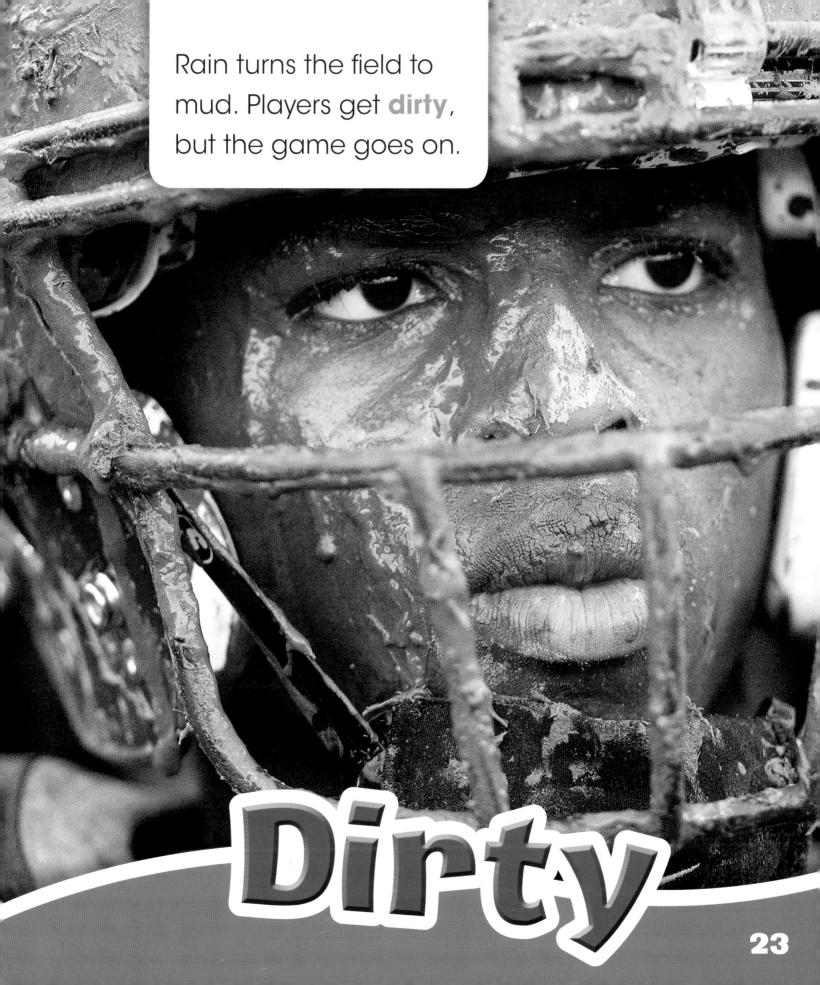

Rain turns the field to mud. Players get **dirty**, but the game goes on.

Dirty

# Long

Some players have **long** hair. It spills out of their helmets and down their backs.

Other players have **short** hair. A short hairstyle helps keep players cool.

Short

# Front

Players wear special shirts called jerseys. On the **front** is the player's number.

On the **back** is the same number plus the player's name.

**Back**

# Dry

Coaches stand on the sidelines, cool and **dry**. They watch the game carefully.

Wet

When a team wins, it's time to celebrate. The coach may be **wet**, but he's happy!

# Glossary

**blur**—a shape that is unclear because it is moving too fast

**goalpost**—a post that marks each end of the field; players get points for getting the ball through the goalposts

**injure**—to hurt

**jersey**—a light shirt that is part of a football player's uniform

**running back**—any player who carries the ball out of the backfield

**sideline**—a line that marks the edge of the long side of a football field

**squash**—to press down upon, crush, or flatten

**stadium**—a large building in which sports events are held

**touchdown**—when the ball is carried over the opposing goal line or caught in the end zone; a touchdown is worth six points

# Read More

**Durrie, Karen.** *Football.* Let's Play.
New York: AV2 by Weigl, 2011.

**Schuette, Sarah L.** *Football Frenzy: A Spot-It Challenge.*
Spot It. North Mankato, Minn.: Capstone Press, 2013.

**Wyatt, James.** *Football.* On the Team.
New York: Gareth Stevens Pub., 2012.

# Internet Sites

FactHound offers a safe, fun way to find Internet sites related to this book. All of the sites on FactHound have been researched by our staff.

Here's all you do:

Visit *www.facthound.com*

Type in this code: 9781429699600

 **Super-cool stuff!** Check out projects, games and lots more at **www.capstonekids.com**

# Index